Sunshine

Pupil's Book 4

Ausgabe Bayern

Erarbeitet von
Stefanie Aschkar (Konstanz)
Tanja Beattie (Ebersberg)
Nadine Kerler (Ulm)
Maria Skejic (Frankfurt am Main)
Caroline Tamm (München)

Auf der Grundlage der Ausgabe von
Birgit Hollbrügge
und Ulrike Kraaz

Cornelsen

Symbols

listen to your partner or teacher

listen to the CD

read

talk

play

draw or write

extra

Contents

> **Note**
>
> where = wo
>
> were = war(en)/warst

1 Talk about the picture. Say: *I can see …*

2 Read the speech bubbles with a partner.

3 Talk about holidays. Ask a partner questions.

1 Talk about Emily's timetable. Say: *On Monday, Emily has Maths, …*

2 Listen. What day is it?

Note

Music – Musik
Maths – Mathe

Science

Music

German

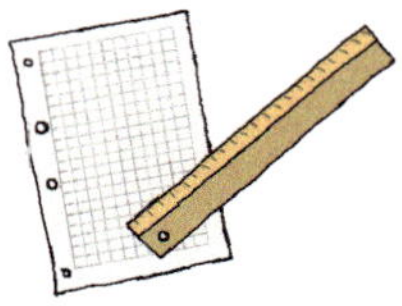

Maths

Time	Monday	Tuesday	Wednesday	Thursday	Friday
9.00-9.30	ASSEMBLY				
9.30-10.30	Maths	Maths	English	Music	Maths
10.30-10.45	PLAY				
10.45-11.45	English	German	Maths	Maths	English
11.45-1.00	LUNCH				
1.00-1.15	QUIET				
1.15-2.15	Music	Computers	Science	English	Art
2.15-3.15	German	P.E.	P.E.	Art	Computers

P.E. (Physical Education)

English

Art

Computers

A trip to London

1 Talk about the map. What can you see?

2 Read the texts. Find the sights on the map.
Say: *Number 1 is...*

(1) **Tower Bridge** is a very famous bridge. It can open to let big ships through. It takes about 90 seconds to open.

(2) **London Zoo** is one of the oldest zoos in the world. You can see about 750 different kinds of animals there.

(3) **Buckingham Palace** is the Queen's London home. On top of Buckingham Palace you can see the Union flag.

(4) **Big Ben** is the name of a bell. The bell is inside the clock tower of Westminster Palace.

Note

The London underground is called the "Tube".

Note
Find out more about the sights 7 and 8.

3 Look at the map.
Listen and find the way.

☆ Say where and when they go.
How do they get there?

(5) The **London Eye** is the biggest observation wheel in the world. It is 135 metres high.

(6) **Madame Tussaud's** is a famous wax museum. You can see film stars, sports stars, pop stars and the Royal Family there. Who is your favourite star?

Let's talk

4 Read the dialogue. Talk to a partner.

☆ More: Make up your own dialogue.

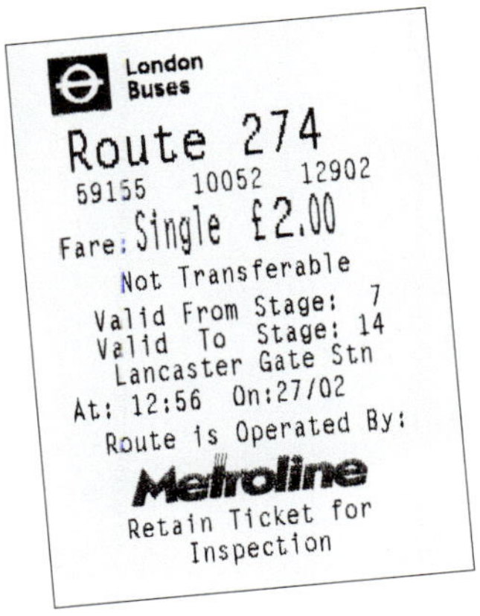
London Buses
Route 274
59155 10052 12902
Fare: Single £2.00
Not Transferable
Valid From Stage: 7
Valid To Stage: 14
Lancaster Gate Stn
At: 12:56 On:27/02
Route is Operated By:
Metroline
Retain Ticket for Inspection

1 Look at the pictures. Talk about the pictures.

2 Read the postcards. Say the numbers.

☆ When was Harry's birthday?
What's the name of Harry's grandma?

Note

Look at Kate's SMS.
What does she write?

Hello Jack,

I'm in London with Kate and her dad.
It's super! Thursday was my birthday.
We went on a boat trip on the River
Thames to the London Eye. It was
great. I could see Buckingham Palace
from the top of the London Eye.

Harry

Dear Grandma,

How are you? I'm in London with my friend Kate and her dad.
It's Tuesday. London is great.
I like sitting at the top of the red buses. Here's a picture of Big Ben. Big Ben is a bell inside the clock tower!

I hope you come to my birthday party on Sunday.

Love, Harry

Mrs Benson
5 Birch Street
Portsmouth
Hants PO12 2TB

Dear Mum,

I like London. It's great!
Yesterday it was Harry's birthday.
Today we went to Hyde Park to eat some ice cream and to play football.
We walked over Tower Bridge, too.
What a big bridge! You must go and see Tower Bridge. It opens in the middle. See you on Saturday.

Love, Kate

Mrs William
12 Morgan Street
Band

Story: **The Earl of Sandwich**

1 Listen to the story.

2 Read the dialogue.

3 Act it out.

Note

Who was the Earl of Sandwich? Find out more!

More to explore: **The Royal Family**

Note

In which other countries are there still kings or queens? Find out!

1 Listen. Point to the pictures.

2 Read the sentences.

People in Britain love the Royal Family.

Royal guards in front of Buckingham Palace.

The Royals are everywhere.

3 Read the sentences. Find the right pictures.

☆ Talk about activities and times. Say: *At 10 a.m. William ...*

One day in the life of two Royals.

Note

a.m. = vormittags
p.m. = nachmittags

08:00 a.m.	Kate takes her dog for a walk.
10:00 a.m.	William visits a football team.
12:00	Kate and William have lunch.
02:00 p.m.	Kate visits pupils at a London school.
07:30 p.m.	Kate and William are at a concert.

All year round

1 What's the weather like? Say: *In picture 1 it's snowy ...*

2 Read the sentences. Talk about the pictures.

It's snowy today.
Nice weather for
my snowman.

It's foggy in London.

Note

Wetterwörter und andere Adjektive enden im Englischen oft auf ein 'y'.

sun – sunn**y**

wind – wind**y**

What a windy day!

It's sunny.

What a rainy day!

Look, it's very cloudy today.
It's going to rain.

Let's talk

1 Read the dialogue. Talk to a partner.
☆ More: Make up your own dialogue.

2 Look at the pictures. Talk to a partner. Say: *In Rome it's …*

1

Rome (15°C)

2

New York (3°C)

3

4

Paris (25°C)

5

Ankara (33°C)

6

London (13°C)

1 Read and match.

My birthday is in spring.

Hi, I'm Robin. My birthday is in September, in autumn. In autumn, the leaves turn red and yellow. When it is windy, I like flying my kite. Do you like my birthday cake?

Hello, my name is Mona. I was born in summer, in July. When it is sunny and hot, I like eating ice cream. What do you do in summer?

Hi, I'm Arian. My birthday is in April, in spring. In spring, there are lots of flowers. I like looking for Easter eggs. Do you like my tree?

Hello, my name is Mathilda. My birthday is in winter, in February. Sometimes it is cold and snowy on my birthday. I like playing in the snow. Do you like my snowman?

2 Answer the questions.

- When is Robin's / Arian's / … birthday? Say: *Robin's birthday is in …*
- What's the weather like in spring / summer / …? Say: *In spring it's …*
- What do the children like? Say: *Robin likes …*
- What about you? Say: *My birthday is in …*

1 Read the texts. Play the game.

START	1 Go forward 2.	2 It's a snowy Saturday in January.	3	4	5 Snowdrops in winter.	6
7 A birthday in March.	8	9 Daffodils in spring.	10	11 25° on Sunday.	12 A rainy Monday in June.	13 Go back 3.
14 A cold Tuesday in summer.	15	16 Throw again.	17 Red roses in July.	18	19 Summer holidays!	20 A sunny Wednesday in August.
21	22 A cloudy Friday in September.	23 A windy Thursday in October.	24 Spiders in autumn.	25	26 Miss a turn.	27 A foggy Monday in November.
28	29 15° on Christmas Day.	30	FINISH			

A snowy Saturday in January.	Go back 1.	Summer holidays!	Throw again.
Snowdrops in winter.	Go forward 1.	A sunny Wednesday in August.	Go forward 1.
A birthday in March.	Go forward 3.	A cloudy Friday in September.	Miss a turn.
Daffodils in spring.	Go forward 2.	A windy Thursday in October.	Go back 2.
25° on Sunday.	Throw again.	Spiders in autumn.	Go forward 2.
A rainy Monday in June.	Go back 2.	A foggy Monday in November.	Miss a turn.
A cold Tuesday in summer.	Miss a turn.	15° on Christmas Day.	Go back 3.

1 Talk about the pictures.
When is the wind helpful? When is the wind dangerous?

2 Read the rhyme.
Say the rhyme.

The kites go up, the kites go down.
See how they fly all over the town.
The children run and jump and play,
Because they love a windy day.

You need:

a glass bottle

a candle

matches

3 Do the experiment with your teacher.

1 Put the candle behind the bottle.
2 Blow hard on the bottle. What happens to the candle?

→ DVD

3 At the museum

1 What animals are in the museum? Say: *There's …*

2 Read the speech bubbles. Talk to a partner.

This is the Natural History Museum in London.

Let's talk

3 Read the dialogue. Talk to a partner.
☆ More: Make your own dialogue.

> **Note**
>
> Say: *no – know*
> Check with your teacher.

1 Read the texts. Which animal is it?

☆ Think of one more animal.
Talk, draw or show.

They live in the jungle.
They eat leaves and grass.
They have got big ears.
They have got two long teeth.
They have got small eyes.
They have got big legs and feet.

They live underground.
They eat snails and worms.
They have got small eyes,
a short tail and
black fur.
They are blind.

They have got small ears.
They have got long arms.
They have got two legs.
They have got long tails.
They live in trees.
They eat bananas and leaves.

2 Read the presentation rules.

 Make notes.

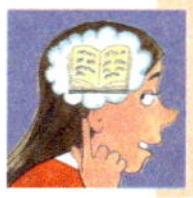 Know your text.

 Speak loudly.

 Look at the class.

 Show pictures.

1 Talk about the pictures.

2 Read the speech bubbles.

Complete the speech bubbles. Work with a partner.

More to explore: **The Jurassic Coast**

1 Listen. Point to the pictures.

2 Read the texts.

> **Note**
>
> What was the biggest, smallest, fastest, heaviest, longest dinosaur? Find out!

1

Jurassic coast

The Jurassic coast is a region in south England.

2

dinosaur fossil

3

dinosaur footprints

4

ammonites

5

a fish

6

dinosaur museum

At the dinosaur museum in Dorchester you can learn a lot about dinosaurs.

Note

Viele englische Schulkinder besuchen während oder nach der Schule einen Klub. Gibt es Klubs oder etwas Ähnliches auch an deiner Schule?

1 Read the posters. Name the club.

2 Work with a partner. Talk about the clubs.

3 Listen. Which club do the children want to go to?

Where's the dance club?

It's in …

When's the … club?

It's on …

1 Listen. What can Linda do?

2 Read the dialogue with a partner.

Make up your own dialogue.

Story: **Giraffes can't dance**

1 Listen. Point to the pictures.

2 Read the story.

Gerald the giraffe likes dancing. But when he dances, his legs get in the way and he falls down.

The other animals laugh at Gerald. They shout out: "Giraffes can't dance!" Poor Gerald! He leaves the dance floor. He is sad and lonely.

A cricket sees Gerald and says: "Don't be sad. You can dance! Everyone can dance. Just listen to the music around you!"

Gerald listens to the music. His legs start to move and then his neck starts to sway. Gerald is so excited. "I can dance. I can dance." He feels wonderful.

The other animals see Gerald dancing. They start to clap. "Wow, Gerald, you are a really good dancer!" they say. Gerald is so proud that he can dance. "Thank you, thank you!" he says. Now all the animals are his friends. He is very happy.

1 Listen and point to the pictures.

1 

2 

3 

4 

Note

Viele englische Kinder spielen *Rounders* auf dem Schulhof. Kennst du ein ähnliches Spiel?

2 Look at the pictures. Read the rules. Talk to a partner about the rules.

You need:

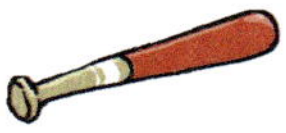 a bat	 a ball	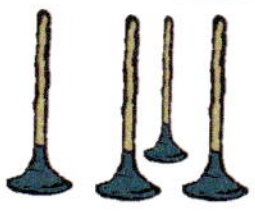 4 posts	 6-15 players

① Form two teams.

batting team

fielding team

② Choose a bowler.

bowler

③ The bowler bowls the ball.
The batter hits the ball.

④ The batter runs from post to post.

The team with the most rounders wins.

 → DVD

1 Talk about the picture.
What are the friends doing?

2 Read the questions.

3 Answer the questions.

What's your name?	*Kate*
How old are you?	*I'm 10 years old.*
When's your birthday?	*May* 26
Where are you from?	*I'm from Great Britain.*
What's your nickname?	*Kitty*
What's your password?	*supergirl*
What are your hobbies?	*dancing, swimming*

Note

Americans pay with dollars ($) and cents.
How much is 1 € in $?

1 Talk about the pictures.

(1)

Statue of Liberty

(2)

Empire State Building

(3)

Central Park

(4)

Brooklyn Bridge

(4)

Yellow cab

2 Listen to Matt's rap. Point to the pictures.

3 Read the text.

Do the rap.

1.
Welcome to New York
Welcome to the sights
Welcome to the city
That never sleeps at night.

2.
Go to Central Park
Have a picnic in the sun
Walk, skate or play
Have lots of fun.

New York City is the place 2 B.
New York City is the place 4 me.
Yo!

3.
The Empire State Building
Is very, very high
It's got a hundred an'
two floors all in all.

4.
Over Brooklyn Bridge
You can bike, walk or ride
Or take a yellow cab
From side to side.

5.
One more sight
You have to see
And that's the famous
Statue of Liberty.

1 Read Kate's email. What does she write about?

To: mattman@world.e-pals.com
Subject: About my family

Dear Matt,
Today I want to write about my family. I live with my mum and dad. Where do you live? Do you have a big family?
My dad has got a second-hand shop. My mum is a hairdresser.
I've got a sister. She's older than me. She's a shop assistant.
I haven't got a brother, but I've got a lot of friends.
My best friends are Harry, Samir and Emily. We like playing in Harry's garden and in the street. What do you like doing?
My grandmother lives in London. I love London. There's so much to see there. I went there in September with Harry and my dad.

What's your family like?

2 Listen to Matt's email.

3 Read the text.

To: kitty@world.e-pals.com
Subject: About me

Hi Kate,
Thanks for your email. I'm ten years old.
My birthday is in November.
I've got a brother. He's a mechanic. And I've got a little sister. My mother is a teacher. My father works in the city. He's a taxi driver. I've got two hamsters.
I like playing with my hamsters.
My hobbies are playing computer games and reading. What are your hobbies?

From,
Matt

Note

What's your mum's or dad's job? Look in a dictionary.

Story: **A day in New York**

1 Talk about the pictures.

2 Read the text.

→ DVD

1 Read the texts about John, the police officer.

2 Listen to your partner. Point to the right picture.

1

2

3

Hello, my name is John.
I'm a police officer
in New York City.

In the city
we patrol by car.

You can go
very fast on a motorbike.

In Central Park
we use horses.

I can see more
from a helicopter.

Do you like my badge?

4

5

6

3 Read the dialogue. Talk to a partner.

More: Make up your own dialogue.

1 Read the story.

6
Do you know a rhyme?
Of course, we do!
I can say: The elephant goes like this and that.
7
I'm very angry. What a bad class.
8
Can you read?
Of course, we can!
I know a story about Gerald the Giraffe.
9
That was bad!
No, that isn't right, inspector.
10
I'm not the school inspector. Sorry, Mrs Brown.
He's the caretaker!
He isn't the school inspector.
11
What a nice class, Mrs Brown!
Thank you, Ms Honey. They're good pupils.

1 What did you learn?
What can you say in English?
Read the texts.

2 Talk about the units.

I know the colours and numbers in English.

I can talk about my family and friends.

I can say which pets I like.

I can talk about my school things.

I can talk about clothes.

I can talk about rooms and furniture.

I can buy food and drinks.

I can read a story book.

How did

That was OK.

That was not so good.

That was great!

I can say what time it is.

I can talk about the weather, seasons and my birthday month.

you like it?

I like …

I don't like … because …

My favourite words are …

I was good at …

I want to learn more about …

I can do a presentation about animals.

I can say what my hobbies are.

I can read the story about Gerald the giraffe.

I can write about myself and my family.

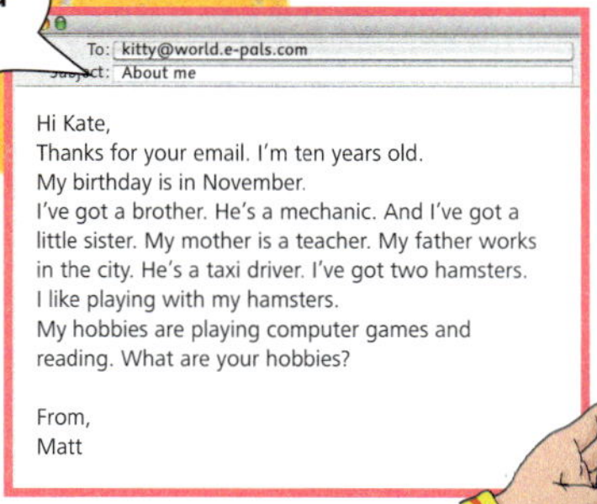
To: kitty@world.e-pals.com
Subject: About me

Hi Kate,
Thanks for your email. I'm ten years old.
My birthday is in November.
I've got a brother. He's a mechanic. And I've got a little sister. My mother is a teacher. My father works in the city. He's a taxi driver. I've got two hamsters.
I like playing with my hamsters.
My hobbies are playing computer games and reading. What are your hobbies?

From,
Matt

I know about Halloween.

1 Read the rhyme, the chant and the rap.

The elephant

The elephant goes
Like this, like that.
He's terribly big,
And he's terribly fat.
He has no fingers,
He has big toes,
And goodness gracious,
What a nose!

Holidays

I was in London,
She was in Rome,
He was in Ankara,
And where were you?
I was at home.

London

Rome

Ankara

Matt's rap

Welcome to New York
Welcome to the sights
Welcome to the city
That never sleeps at nights.

Go to Central Park
Have a picnic in the sun
Walk, skate or play
Have lots of fun.

New York City is the place to be
New York City is the place for me.
Yo!

1 Talk about the picture.

How many ghosts, monsters, pumpkins, skeletons, ... can you see?

2 Listen to the rhymes.

3 Read the rhymes.

Special Days: **Bonfire Night**

1 Talk about the pictures.

2 Listen to the rhyme.

3 Read the rhyme.

☆ Say the rhyme.

Remember, remember
The fifth of November,
Gunpowder, treason and plot.
I see no reason
Why gunpowder treason
Should ever be forgot.

1

2

3

4

Special Days: **Christmas**

1 Listen to the story. Point to the pictures.

2 Read the story.

☆ Sing the song. Find the matching pictures.

Rudolph is a reindeer. He has a red and shiny nose.

The other reindeer laugh at Rudolph's nose.

Poor Rudolph is sad and lonely.

It's Christmas Eve. It's very foggy. Santa asks Rudolph for help.

Rudoph helps Santa. He guides the sleigh. He shows the reindeer the way.

Rudolf is very proud and very happy. The reindeer are his friends. They all love him. Rudolf is never sad and lonely again.

Looking at English

So verändern sich die Wörter in der Mehrzahl:
Wenn du von mehreren Dingen sprichst, hängst du ein ‚s' an.

one book – two book**s**
one apple – two apple**s**

➜ Es gibt Ausnahmen, die du dir merken musst:

one child- two child**ren**
one hobb**y** – two hobb**ies**

Note

Finde Beispiele in deinem Pupil's Book!

So sagst du, dass jemanden etwas gehört:

This is Tim**'s** book.

This is Anne**'s** pencil case.

Diese Wörter brauchst du, um Fragen zu stellen:

What? = Was?
What is this? Was ist das?

When? = Wann?
When is your birthday?

Where? = Wo?
Where is my book?

Who? = Wer
Who is on the phone??

How? = Wie?
How are you?

How many? = Wie viele?
How many children like chocolate?

How much? = Wie viel?
How much is the orange juice?

➜ Es gibt Ausnahmen, die du dir merken musst:

How much is …? = Was kostet …?
What time is it? = Wie spät ist es?
What's your name? = Wie heißt du?

So fangen viele Fragen an:

Do you like …? = Magst du …?
Can I have …? = Kann ich … haben?
Have you got …? = Hast du …?
Are you happy/sad/angry? = Bist du glücklich, traurig, wütend?

Looking at English

So kannst du über dich und andere sprechen:

I am

you are

he is

she is

it is

we are

you are

they are

Manche Wörter werden abgekürzt:

I am = I'm
you are = you're
he is = he's
she is = she's
it is = it's
we are = we're
you are = you're
they are = they're

I can = I can't
where is = where's
what is = what's
I would like = I'd like
I have got = I've got

Note

Finde Beispiele in deinem Pupil's Book!

Manche Wörter haben mehrere Bedeutungen:

you	=	du, ihr, sie
it	=	er, sie, es

Word list

Englisch–Deutsch

A

about über

again noch einmal, wieder

angry verärgert

animal Tier

answer antworten, Lösung

Art Kunst (Schulfach)

ask fragen

at bei, im, um

autumn Herbst

B

back Rücken

bad schlecht

ballet Ballett

basketball Basketball

be sein

because weil

behind hinter

belly Bauch

bend beugen

big groß

birthday Geburtstag

blackboard Tafel

blow out auspusten

boat Boot

bonfire Lagerfeuer

book Buch

boy Junge

bread Brot

brother Bruder

bus Bus

bus driver Busfahrer/in

bush Busch

but aber

butter Butter

buy kaufen

C

calendar Kalender

camel Kamel

can können

candle Kerze

car Auto

caretaker Hausmeister

chair Stuhl

cent (hier: amerikanischer) Cent

cheese Käse

chicken Huhn

chips Pommes Frites

chocolate Schokolade

Christmas Weihnachten

city Großstadt

clap klatschen

class Klasse

classroom Klassenraum

clock Uhr

clock tower Glockenturm

cloudy wolkig

club AG, Klub, Verein

colour Farbe, ausmalen

come kommen

Computers Computer (Schulfach)

crocodile Krokodil

cut out ausschneiden

D

daffodil Osterglocke

dance tanzen

dangerous gefährlich

day Tag

Dear ... Liebe/r ...

degree(s) Grad

dinosaur Dinosaurier

do machen, tun

do ballet Ballett tanzen

do judo Judo betreiben

dollar ($) (hier: amerikanischer) Dollar

door Tür

down, downstairs unten

draw zeichnen

dream Traum

drink trinken, Getränk

driver Fahrer

E

ear Ohr

eat essen

egg Ei

elephant Elefant

email E-Mail

England England

English englisch, Englisch (Schulfach)

e-pal E-Mail-Freund/in

euro (€) Euro

eye Auge

F

famous berühmt

father Vater

Father Christmas Weihnachtsmann
favourite Lieblings-
feed füttern
fireworks Feuerwerk
flag Flagge
flap auf und ab bewegen
fly fliegen
foggy neblig
food Essen
foot, feet Fuß, Füße
football Fußball
forget vergessen
forward vorwärts
Friday Freitag
from aus, von

G

game Spiel
German deutsch, Deutsch (Schulfach)
Germany Deutschland
ghost Geist
giraffe Giraffe
girl Mädchen
give geben
glue kleben
go gehen
Good luck! Viel Glück!
Goodness gracious! Du meine Güte!
grandfather, grandpa Großvater, Opa
grandmother, grandma Großmutter, Oma
Great Britain Großbritannien
gunpowder Schießpulver

H

hairdresser Friseur/in
half past/to halb (Uhrzeit)
Halloween Halloween
ham Schinken
happen geschehen
happy glücklich
have (got) haben
have to müssen
he er
head Kopf
hello Hallo
help helfen, Hilfe
helpful hilfreich
her ihr/ihre
here hier
hippo Nilpferd
his sein/seine
hobby Hobby
holidays Ferien
(at) home zuhause
hop hopsen, springen
hope hoffen
horse Pferd
hot heiß, warm
house Haus
how wie
how many wie viele
how much wie viel

I

idea Idee
ill krank
in in
in front of vor
inspector Inspektor/in, Schulrat/rätin
is ist
it es

J

job Beruf, Job
judo Judo
jump springen
jungle Dschungel

K

king König
kite Drachen
knee Knie
know kennen, wissen

L

late spät
leaf, leaves Blatt, Blätter
left links
leg Bein
lesson Schulstunde
Let's go! Los!
lettuce Kopfsalat
line Linie, Reihe
lion Löwe
listening to music Musik hören
little klein
live leben, wohnen
long lang
look at betrachten

Word list

loud, loudly laut
love lieben
Love, ... Liebe Grüße ...

M

make machen
many viel/e
matches Streichhölzer
Maths Mathe (Schulfach)
mechanic Mechaniker/in
meeting friends Freunde treffen
miss a turn aussetzen
Monday Montag
monkey Affe
morning Morgen
mother Mutter
motorbike Motorrad
move (sich) bewegen
much viel
museum Museum
Music Musik (Schulfach)
my mein

N

name Name
next to neben
nice nett
nickname Spitzname
nose Nase
not nicht
notes Noten
number Nummer

O

o'clock ...Uhr
of course natürlich
old alt
on auf
open offen

P

P.E. (= Physical Education) Sport (Schulfach)
paper Papier
parrot Papagei
password Passwort
photo Foto
picture Bild
plane Flugzeug
play spielen, Theaterspiel
please bitte
plot Verschwörung
point to auf ... zeigen
police officer Polizist/in
police station Polizeiwache
postcard Postkarte
present Geschenk
pumpkin Kürbis
pupil Schüler/in
put legen, stellen

Q

quarter past/to viertel nach/vor (Uhrzeit)
Queen Königin
quiet leise

R

rainy regnerisch
read lesen
remember erinnern
rhyme Reim
ride a horse reiten
right rechts
river Fluss
rose Rose
run laufen

S

sad traurig
salad (zubereiteter) Salat
Santa, Santa Claus Weihnachtsmann (in den USA)
Saturday Samstag
savannah Savanne
say sagen
scared verängstigt
Science Naturwissenschaften, Heimat- und Sachunterricht (Schulfach)
sea Meer
season Jahreszeit
see sehen
she sie
shop assistant Verkäufer/in
short kurz
shoulder Schulter
show zeigen
sight Sehenswürdigkeit
sing singen
sister Schwester
sit sitzen

skeleton Skelett
ski Ski, Ski fahren
small klein
snake Schlange
snap schnipsen
snowdrop Schneeglöckchen
snowy verschneit
speak sprechen
spider Spinne
sports Sportarten
spring Frühling
stamp aufstampfen
star Star
street Straße
stretch dehnen, strecken
strong stark
subject Fach, Schulfach
summer Sommer
Sunday Sonntag
sunny sonnig
sweets Süßigkeiten
swim schwimmen

T

table Tisch
table tennis Tischtennis
tail Schwanz
talk reden
taxi Taxi
taxi driver Taxifahrer/in
tea Tee
teacher Lehrer/in
temperature Temperatur
tennis Tennis
text message, SMS SMS
there dort
they sie
this diese/r/s
throw werfen
Thursday Donnerstag
ticket Fahrkarte
tiger Tiger
time Zeit
timetable Stundenplan
to nach, zu
today heute
toe Zeh
toilet Toilette
tomato Tomate
tooth, teeth Zahn, Zähne
touch anfassen, berühren
train Zug
treason Verrat
tree Baum
Tuesday Dienstag
tummy Bauch
turn abbiegen
turn around umdrehen
tusk Rüssel

U

under unter
underground U-Bahn
understand verstehen
up, upstairs oben
USA USA (= Vereinigte Staaten von Amerika)
useful nützlich

V

Vampire Vampir

W

walk gehen
want wollen
watching TV Fernsehen
water Wasser
we wir
weather Wetter
weather report Wetterbericht
Wednesday Mittwoch
weekend Wochenende
welcome willkommen
whale Wal
what was
wheel Rad
when wann
where wo
who wer
why warum
wiggle hin- und her bewegen, zappeln
wild wild
windy windig
winter Winter
wish wünschen
witch Hexe

A
abbiegen turn
Affe monkey
alt old
anfassen touch
anschauen look at
antworten answer
auf on
auf und ab bewegen flap
aufstampfen stamp
auf … zeigen point to
Auge eye
aus from
ausmalen colour
ausschneiden cut out
aussetzen miss a turn
Auto car

B
Ballett ballet
Ballett machen do ballet
Basketball basketball
Bauch belly, tummy
Baum tree
bei at
Bein leg
Beruf job
beugen bend
berühmt famous
berühren touch
(sich) bewegen move
Bild picture
bitte please
Blatt, Blätter leaf, leaves
Boot boat
Brot bread
Bruder brother
Buch book
Bus bus
Busch bush
Busfahrer/in bus driver
Butter butter

C
Cent cent
Computer (Schulfach) Computers

D
dehnen stretch
Deutsch (Schulfach) German
Deutschland Germany
Dienstag Tuesday
diese/r/s this
Dinosaurier dinosaur
Dollar ($) dollar ($)
Donnerstag Thursday
dort there
Drachen kite
Dschungel jungle
Du meine Güte! Goodness gracious!

E
Ei egg
Elefant elephant
E-mail email
E-mail-Freund/in e-pal
England England
Englisch (Schulfach) English
er he
erinnern remember
es it
essen eat
Essen food
Euro (€) euro

F
Fach, Schulfach subject
Fahrer driver
Fahrkarte ticket
Farbe colour
Ferien holidays
fernsehen watching TV
Feuerwerk fireworks
Flagge flag
fliegen fly
Flugzeug plane
Fluss river
Foto photo
fragen ask
Freitag Friday
Freunde treffen meeting friends
Friseur/in hairdresser
Frühling spring
Fuß, Füße foot, feet
Fußball football
füttern feed

G
geben give
gefährlich dangerous
gehen go, walk
Geist ghost

geschehen happen
Geschenk present
Getränk drink
Giraffe giraffe
Glockenturm clock tower
glücklich happy
Grad degree(s)
groß big
Großbritannien Great Britain
Großmutter, Oma grandmother, grandma
Großstadt city
Großvater, Opa grandfather, grandpa

H

haben have (got)
halb (Uhrzeit) half past/to
Hallo hello
Halloween Halloween
Haus house
Hausmeister caretaker
Heimat- und Sachunterricht (Schulfach) Science
heiß hot
helfen help
Herbst autumn
heute today
Hexe witch
hier here
hin und her bewegen, zappeln wiggle
Hilfe help
hilfreich helpful
Hobby hobby
hoffen hope
hopsen hop
Huhn chicken

I

Idee idea
ihr, ihre her, its
in in
ist is

J

Jahreszeit season
Job job
Judo judo
Judo betreiben do judo

K

Kalender calendar
Kamel camel
Käse cheese
kaufen buy
kennen know
Klasse class
Klassenraum classroom
klatschen clap
kleben glue
Klebstift glue stick
Kleid dress
klein little, small
Klub, AG club
Knie knee
kommen come
König king
Königin queen
können can
Kopf head
Kopfsalat lettuce
krank ill
Krokodil crocodile
Kunst (Schulfach) Art
Kürbis pumpkin
kurz short

L

Lagerfeuer bonfire
lang long
laufen run
laut loud, loudly
leben, wohnen live
legen put
Lehrer/in teacher
leise quiet
lesen read
Liebe/r … Dear …
Liebe Grüße … Love, …
lieben love
Lieblings- favourite
Linie line
links left
Los! Let's go!
Löwe lion

M

machen do, make
Mathe (Schulfach) Maths
Mechaniker/in mechanic
Meer sea
mein my

Word list

Mittwoch Wednesday
Montag Monday
Morgen morning
Motorrad motorbike
Museum museum
Musik (Schulfach) Music
Musik hören istening to music
müssen have to
Mutter mother

N

nach, zu to
Name name
Nase nose
natürlich of course
Naturwissenschaften (Schulfach) Science
neben next to
neblig foggy
nett nice
nicht not
Nilpferd hippo
noch einmal again
Noten notes
Nummer number
nützlich useful

O

oben upstairs
offen open
Ohr ear
Oma grandma
Opa grandpa
Osterglocke daffodil

P

Papagei parrot
Papier paper
Passwort password
Pferd horse
Polizeiwache police station
Polizist/in police officer
Pommes Frites chips
Postkarte postcard

R

Rad wheel
rechts right
reden talk
regnerisch rainy
Reihe line
Reim rhyme
reiten ride a horse
Rose rose
Rücken back
Rüssel tusk

S

sagen say
Salat (zubereitet) salad
Samstag Saturday
Savanne savannah
Schießpulver gunpowder
Schinken ham
Schlange snake
schlecht bad
Schneeglöckchen snowdrop
schnipsen snap
Schokolade chocolate
Schüler/in pupil
Schulfach (school) subject
Schulstunde lesson
Schulter shoulder
Schwanz tail
Schwester sister
schwimmen swim
sehen look, see
Sehenswürdigkeit sight
sein be
sein/e his
sein, ihr its
sie she, they
singen sing
sitzen sit
Skelett skeleton
Ski, Ski fahren ski
SMS SMS, text message
snap schnipsen
Sommer summer
sonnig sunny
Sonntag Sunday
spät late
Spiel game
spielen play
Spinne spider
Spitzname nickname
Sport (Schulfach) P.E. (= Physical Education)
Sportarten sports
sprechen speak
springen jump

Star star
stark strong
stellen put
Straße street
strecken stretch
Stuhl chair
Stundenplan timetable
Süßigkeiten sweets

T

Tafel blackboard
Tag day
tanzen dance
Taxi taxi
Taxifahrer/in taxi driver
Tee tea
Temperatur temperature
Tennis tennis
Theaterspiel play
Tier animal
Tiger tiger
Tisch table
Tischtennis table tennis
Toilette toilet
Tomate tomato
Traum dream
traurig sad
trinken drink
Tür door

U

U-Bahn underground
über about
Uhr clock, ... o'clock
um at
umdrehen turn around
unten down, downstairs
unter under
USA (Vereinigte Staaten von Amerika) USA

V

Vampir vampire
Vater father
verängstigt scared
verärgert angry
vergessen forget
Verkäufer/in shop assistant
Verrat treason
verschneit snowy
Verschwörung plot
verstehen understand
viel much
viel/e many
Viel Glück! Good luck!
viertel vor/nach (Uhrzeit) quarter to/past
von from
vor in front of
vorwärts forward

W

Wal whale
wann when
warm hot
warum why
was what
Wasser water
Weihnachten Christmas
Weihnachtsmann Father Christmas, Santa Claus (USA)
weil because
wer who
werfen throw
Wetter weather
Wetterbericht weather report
wie how
wie viel how much
wie viele how many
wild wild
Willkommen welcome
windig windy
Winter winter
wir we
wissen know
wo where
Wochenende weekend
wohnen live
wolkig cloudy
wollen want
wünschen wish

Z

Zahn, Zähne tooth, teeth
Zeh toe
zeichnen draw
zeigen show
Zeit time
zu to
Zug train
zuhause (at) home

Sunshine

Lehrwerk für den früh beginnenden Englischunterricht

Pupil's Book 4

Ausgabe Bayern

Erarbeitet von
Stefanie Aschkar, Konstanz; Tanja Beattie, Ebersberg; Nadine Kerler, Ulm; Maria Skejic, Frankfurt am Main; Caroline Tamm, München

Auf der Grundlage der Ausgabe von
Birgit Hollbrügge, Bielefeld; Ulrike Kraaz, Werther

Beratende Mitwirkung
Uwe Becker, Mannheim; Margit Butscher-Wich, Bad Abbach; Michael Duscha, Braunschweig; Renate Hafner, Blaustein; Siân Williams-Hahn, Schorndorf (englischsprachige Texte)

Verlagsredaktion
Daniela Aue

Illustration
Beehive Illustration, Circencester, England; Mike Phillipps, Neil Chapman; Volker Fredrich, Hamburg; Mary Hall, Bath, England

Umschlaggestaltung und Layout
Corinna Babylon, Berlin

Technische Umsetzung
Michaela Müller für agentur corngreen, Leipzig

www.cornelsen.de

1. Auflage, 1. Druck 2015

Alle Drucke dieser Auflage sind inhaltlich unverändert und können im Unterricht nebeneinander verwendet werden.

Druck: Stürz GmbH, Würzburg

ISBN 978-3-06-083852-3

Quellenangaben

Bilder: akg-images (S. 9/Bild 02 John Montagu, 4th Earl of Sandwich: IAM); Daniela Aue, Berlin (S. 13/Bilder 03-06 Kinder; S. 15/Bild 08 Mädchen); culture-images (S. 16/Bild 03 Natural History Museum: The Natural History Museum; S. 20/Bild 06 Fisch: The Natural History Museum); F1 online (S. 10/Bild 05 Guards); Fotolia (S. 3/Bild 03, S. 5/Bild 02 Rucksack: design56; S. 3/Bild 05, S. 9/Bild 01 Käse: pinkcoala; S. 3/Bild 06, S. 6, S. 7, S. 8/Bild 02, S. 10/Bild 02 Bus: Ludmila Smite; S. 3/Bild 07, S. 10/Bild 03 Uhr: cobalt; S. 3/Bild 09, S. 11, S. 12, S. 13/Bild 02, S. 14/Bild 02, S. 15/Bild 01 Blatt: Africa Studio; S. 3/Bild 15, S. 21/Bild 02, S. 22, S. 24/Bild 01 Fußball: Andrey Kiselev; S. 3/Bild 17, S. 28/Bild 01, S. 29/Bild 01 Kamm und Schere: odluap; S. 3/Bild 18, S. 26/Bild 01, S. 26/Bild 02, S. 28/Bild 02, S. 29/Bild 02 Statue of Liberty: LittleSteven65; S. 3/Bild 19, S. 25, S. 27/Bild 02 Computertasten: momius; S. 3/Bild 23, S. 35 Kürbis: Pioppo; S. 8/Bild 03 Big Ben: chrisdorney; S. 8/Bild 04 Tower Bridge: sborisov; S. 12/Bild 05 Paris: anmalkov; S. 12/Bild 06, S. 34/Bild 03 Ankara: Senicer; S. 12/Bild 07, S. 34/Bild 01 London: Bikeworldtravel; S. 15/Bild 03 Unwetter am Pier: fotoart-wallraf; S. 15/Bild 04 Tornado: Chris White; S. 15/Bild 05 Windsurfer: fotografiche.eu; S. 15/Bild 06 Windräder: Gabriel Rohde; S. 15/Bild 07 Sturmschäden: klz; S. 20/Bild 02 Jurrassic Coast: jesshe; S. 24/Bild 02 Hockeyspielerin: Natalia Danecker; S. 26/Bild 03 Empire State Building: rabit75_fot; S. 26/Bild 04 Dollarschein: amgadfoto; S. 26/Bild 05 Cent: rsooll; S. 26/Bild 06 Central Park: pio3; S. 26/Bild 07 Brooklyn Bridge: andreykr; S. 26/Bild 08 Taxi: Andreas Rodriguez; S. 29/Bild 03 New York Police: Dirk Paessler; S. 33/Bild 01 Uhr: Bondarau; GlowImages (S. 3/Bild 02, S. 4 Mädchen: Westend61; S. 3/Bild 04, S. 3/Bild 17, S. 10/Bild 01, S. 27/Bild 01 Familie: Imagesource); S. 36/Bild 02 Puppe: Superstock RM; mauritius images (S. 3/Bild 11, S. 3/Bild 13, S. 18/Bild 02, S. 19/Bild 02, S. 21/Bild 01, S. 23/Bild 02 Füße: Photoshot Creative; S. 12/Bild 02, S. 34/Bild 02 Rom: Alamy; S. 20/Bild 03 Dinosaurier Fossil: Alamy; S. 20/Bild 04 Dinosaurier Fußabdrücke: Alamy; S. 20/Bild 05 Ammoniten: Alamy; S. 24/Bild 03 Cricketspieler: Alamy; S. 24/Bild 04 Rugbyspieler: Alamy; S. 24/Bild 05 Fußballspielerin: Cultura; Photoshot (S. 10/Bild 04 Fans: Xinhua / Yin Gang); © Guy Parker-Rees, Courtesy Orchard Books (S. 23/Bilder 03-08, S. 33/Bild 02); Puppet Empire (S. 10/Bild 08, S. 15/Bild 09, S. 20/Bild 07, S. 20/Bild 08, S. 24/Bild 06): Filmszene aus „Mr. Digger & Mr. Mole“; Reuters (S. 10/Bild 06 Tasse: Suzanne Plunkett); Shutterstock (S. 3/Bild 01, S. 3/Bild 08, S. S. 3/Bild 14, S. 5/Bild 01, S. 8, Bild 01, S. 13/Bild 01, S. 14/Bild 01 Kalender: Mega Pixel); S. 3/Bild 10, S. 16/Bild 01, S. 17/Bild 01, S. 18/Bild 01, S. 19/Bild 01, S. 20/Bild 01, S. 23/Bild 01 Elefant: pandapaw; S. 3/Bild 12, S. 16/Bild 02, S. 17/Bild 02 Verkehrsschild: xtock; S. 3/Bild 21, S. 36/Bild 01, S. 36/Bild 05 Feuerwerk: Steve Allen; S. 8/Bild 05 London Eye: Cedric Weber; S. 10/Bild 07 Prince William und Kate Middleton: Shaun Jeffers; S. 12/Bild 03 New York: Ellen McKnight; S. 12/Bild 04 Wetterübersicht: ojal; S. 15/Bild 02 Kind mit Drachen: Chepko Danil; S. 29/Bild 04 Patch: Al Mueller; S. 29/Bild 05 Helikopter: Scott Lomenzo; S. 29/Bild 06 Polizist: pio3; S. 29/Bild 07 Polizisten auf Pferde: Leonard Zhukovsky; S. 29/Bild 08 Polizisten auf Motorrädern: Leonard Zhukovsky; S. 36/Bild 04 Bonfire: Cristian Gusa; S. 36/Bild 05 Feuerwerk: Steve Allen; vario images (S. 36/Bild 03 Mädchen mit Wunderkerze: Image Source RF); Your photo today. A1 pix – superbild (S. 3/Bild 22, S. 37 Weihnachtszweig)